The Nails and the Cross

THE NAILS AND THE CROSS

Entering into the Mysteries of the Passion

BY GEOFFREY ROWELL AND
JULIEN CHILCOTT-MONK

Pauline
BOOKS & MEDIA
Boston

Library of Congress Cataloging-in-Publication Data

Rowell, Geoffrey.
 [Flesh, bone, wood]
 The nails and the cross : entering into the mysteries of the Passion / by Geoffrey Rowell and Julien Chilcott-Monk.
   p. cm.
 ISBN 0-8198-7411-6
 1. Jesus Christ—Passion—Meditations. 2. Lent—Meditations. I. Chilcott-Monk, J. P. II. Title.
 BT431.3 .R69 2003
 242'.34—dc22

2003018486

The Scripture quotations contained herein are from the *New Revised Standard Version Bible, Catholic Edition,* copyright ©1999, 1995, and 1989 by the Division of Christian Education of the National Council of the Church of Christ in the U.S.A., and are used by permission. All rights reserved.

Cover art: Daughters of St. Paul, U.S.A.
Cover design: Regina Frances Dick, FSP

All rights reserved. No part of this book may be reproduced or transmitted in any form or by any means, electronic or mechanical, including photocopying, recording or by any information storage and retrieval system without permission in writing from the publisher.

Copyright © 2002, by Geoffrey Rowell and Julien Chilcott-Monk
The Author asserts the moral right to be identified as the Author of this Work.

Originally published in English under the title *Flesh, Bone, Wood* by the Canterbury Press Norwich of St. Mary's Works, St. Mary's Plain, Norwich, Norfolk, NR3 3BH, U.K.

2004 Printed and published in the U.S.A. by Pauline Books & Media, 50 Saint Pauls Avenue, Boston, MA 02130-3491.

www.pauline.org

Pauline Books & Media is the publishing house of the Daughters of St. Paul, an international congregation of women religious serving the Church with the communications media.

1 2 3 4 5 6 7 8 9   11 10 09 08 07 06 05 04

Contents

Introduction — VII

Preface and How to Use This Book — XIII

ASH WEDNESDAY TO SATURDAY — 1

LENT I
Colt   Switch   Branch — 17

LENT II
Take   Break   Feed — 37

LENT III
Sweat   Blood   Kiss — 55

LENT IV
Priest   King   Judge — 69

LENT V
Strip   Scourge   Mock — 83

HOLY WEEK
Flesh   Bone   Wood — 99

THE DAY OF RESURRECTION
Christ   Is   Risen — 123

INTRODUCTION

A strong thread running through the spirituality of the seventeenth-century writer Jean-Joseph Surin (1600–1665) was a Passion mysticism, which drew him to focus on the sufferings of Christ as a key to penitence. Thus he could write:

> Let us contemplate the mirror of all the penitent saints: Jesus Christ in the Praetorium of Pilate and upon the cross. In the Praetorium he appears as an object of abomination before the whole people, in the ludicrous regalia of a mock king.... For since an incarnate God was willing to appear in that state in which Pilate showed him to the people, what point would it have if not to say to men, through his example, what St. Ignatius says in his *Constitutions*, that "out of gratitude and love for him, we should desire to be reckoned fools and glory in wearing his livery."[1]

This kind of imaginative contemplation has deep roots in the history of Christian devotion. Surin is an outstanding example, but Ignatius of Loyola, whom he

---

1. J-J. Surin, Letter to Père Huby, quoted in ibid., p. 141.

quotes, is another, whose contemporary influence has been powerful, but whose earlier influence on patterns of meditation and visualization of the Passion in Herbert, Donne, and Crashaw is also notable.[2] As early as the turn of the fifth century, John Cassian brought the monastic traditions of the Christian East to the West, and in his *Conferences* he distilled some of the major themes of the spiritual wisdom he had learned from the fathers of the desert. In that context, as Owen Chadwick has written, the Bible was studied devotionally rather than critically, searching for "what it meant obviously for the characters in the Bible; then what it meant for the soul that reads; and finally what it meant for the Church of all time.... It was intended more to touch the heart than to inform the head."[3]

In the first of his *Conferences,* Cassian writes that "the activity of the heart is compared, not inappropriately, to that of a mill which is activated by the circular motion of water."

---

2. J. A. W. Bennett, *Poetry of the Passion: Studies in Twelve Centuries of English Verse* (Clarendon Press: Oxford, 1982), pp. 145ff.

3. Owen Chadwick, "Introduction to John Cassian: Conferences," *Classics of Western Spirituality* (Paulist Press: New York, 1985), p. 22.

The mill cannot cease operations at all so long as it is driven round by the pressure of the water, and it, then, becomes quite feasible for the person in charge to decide whether he prefers wheat or barley or darnel to be ground. And one thing is clear: only that will be ground which is fed in by the one who is in charge.

To overcome "the lairs of the wild beasts within us and the hiding places of the venomous serpents," we need every hour and every moment to "work over the earth of our heart with the plow of Scripture, that is, with the memory of the Lord's cross."[4]

In the fourteenth century the fire of love that is to be kindled in our hearts was seen as flowing through the Passion of Christ.

The divine fatherly wisdom flows continually through the Passion of our Lord into panting, thirsting hearts which are burned up by the divine fire of love. The first so dries and burns them that they are seized with an excessive thirst, and in this thirst they run with a flaming desire to the streams and to the wounds of

---

4. Cassian, *Conferences,* I.18, 22, pp. 52, 58.

our Lord from which all grace flows. To these they hold their mouths and drink.[5]

Lady Julian, Thomas Traherne, and Isaac Watts—the last through his communion hymn, "When I Survey the Wondrous Cross"—remind us of how universal this imaginative contemplation of the Lord's Passion has been.

Meditation can be described as "a craft of thinking."[6] It has always involved picturing as a way of entering into the story of salvation; and icons, frescoes, stained glass, and the very architecture of churches have been called upon to assist in this process. The tradition of beginning an act of meditation or worship with the sign of the cross is very ancient, and the painted cross, whether on the walls of churches or in the cross-carpet pages of books like the Lindisfarne Gospels (c. 698), acted as a visual marker to lead into prayer.[7]

---

5. *The Book of the Poor in Spirit,* quoted in Kenneth Leech, *True Prayer: An Introduction to Christian Spirituality* (Sheldon Press: London, 1980), p. 38.

6. Mary Carruthers, *The Craft of Thought: Meditation, Rhetoric and the Making of Images, 400–1200* (Cambridge University Press: Cambridge, 1998), p. 4.

7. Ibid., p. 168.

This Lent book, therefore, stands in a long Christian tradition in providing passages of Scripture, together with imaginative reflections from the Beloved Disciple or others involved in the Lord's Passion, to be doors through which we may enter into the saving mystery of the cross. The short passages of comment challenge us to both further meditation and deeper response. The book ends with Easter, for it is in the light of Easter that the cross is seen as the place where God both plumbed the depth of human evil and also "reigned and triumphed from the tree." As two recent writers put it, the Lord "handed himself over without limit or reserve—unto death. He entered into the totality or extremity of passion—the situation in which there is no limit to what may be done to one, to what one may receive or suffer."[8] For that reason:

> Jesus is still and always Jesus crucified. There is no going back on the crucifixion. Jesus does not want it undone; God does not want it undone, because it is in looking at Jesus crucified that we see him in focus,

---

8. W. H. Vanstone, *The Stature of Waiting* (Darton, Longman & Todd: London, 1982), p. 87.

brought to a still point. And as we get Jesus in focus, so through him we see to the heart of God.[9]

And the heart of God is a love that will never let us down and will never let us go.

✠ GEOFFREY ROWELL

---

9. Geoffrey Preston, *Hallowing the Time: Meditations on the Cycle of the Christian Liturgy* (Darton, Longman & Todd: London, 1980), p. 108.

Preface and How to Use This Book

It is our hope that this book of spiritual exercises will encourage a profound contemplation of the Passion of our Lord during the season of Lent; but it is not, perhaps, a conventional Lent book of readings and prayer. For such a book, the reader must look elsewhere. *The Nails and the Cross* follows both the imaginative, meditative tradition of Ignatian spirituality and the much older tradition of memory and meditation explored by my fellow author in the Introduction.

Daily, the reader is invited to enter the period of meditation with material from the book of Lamentations, traditionally used at Tenebrae during Holy Week. It is employed verse by verse from Ash Wednesday to the Saturday before Palm Sunday. Other appropriate verses from Lamentations are used for Holy Week and on Easter Sunday.

The book of Lamentations is a treasure chest. It can profoundly assist in deepening the reader's contemplation of the Passion of our Lord. The author of Lamentations—scholars no longer attribute its authorship to Jeremiah—considers the loss of the kingdom of Judah to Babylon, the despoiling of Jerusalem, and the transportation of its people to Babylon. He considers the sin of God's people and prays for them. Sometimes he writes as an objective observer; sometimes he speaks as Jerusalem herself in the first person. Sometimes he speaks for himself. We can variously apply these words to ourselves in self-examination or in our contemplation of the condition of humanity and of the whole of creation, as a basis for intercession. Sometimes the words will seem to issue out of the very mouth of our rejected Savior himself.

In meditating upon and praying the Lamentations, we place ourselves with those in the Church who have prayed them over the centuries and who do so now, year after year. In this way, each of us prepares to stand beside—or, indeed, in the shoes of—the Beloved Disciple and others, as the crucifixion slowly and agonizingly takes place. And to all of this will be brought our own understanding in the knowledge and light of the Resurrection. Consequently, a picture of the Passion emerges from different perspectives—from different camera angles, as it were. For as long as time allows, the mind ought to be given free rein to enter completely into the drama and pain of the Passion, which is at one with the pain and suffering of a fallen world. And yet, at the heart of the Passion is the mystery of our salvation and healing.

Three psalms—130, 22, and 93—thread their way through Lent after the "soliloquy," and then a reflection and a point under "For further consideration" are provided: for application, self-examination, or consideration. The reflection is meant to elucidate or to open a door to other lines of enquiry; the other not only to stand alone as genuinely arising from what has gone before, but also to serve as a mnemonic with which the reader can associate the various strands of the day's contemplation. The common theme for each week of Lent is summed up in the title of the week. Each successive day the reader should be able to benefit from the cumulative effect of the previous days' contemplation, and so be able to take further steps in the journey toward the foot of the cross.

It is entirely up to the reader, but I suggest that the daily session(s) begin in prayer, for example, the Glory

Be and the Our Father—and end in prayer, for example, a Hail Mary and the Opening Prayer of the day's liturgy. However, something less formal and less rigid may be preferred. To assist in the work of contemplation, it is often helpful to place before oneself a crucifix, icon, or a painting of the Passion.

JULIEN CHILCOTT-MONK

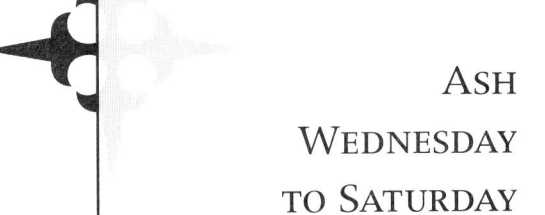

Ash Wednesday to Saturday

Ash Wednesday

Lamentations 1:1–2

How lonely sits the city that once was full of people! How like a widow she has become, she that was great among the nations! She that was a princess among the provinces has become a vassal.

She weeps bitterly in the night, with tears on her cheeks; among all her lovers she has no one to comfort her; all her friends have dealt treacherously with her, they have become her enemies.

The Beloved Disciple (on arrival at Golgotha):

I am watching the final stages of a nightmare. The past hours have made it clear that this hideous drama has now taken on a momentum of its own, as if beyond human control; yes, beyond the control of any of the players: of Annas, Caiaphas, Herod, Pilate, or even Caesar himself. The Master's equanimity seems to be a painful resignation, almost contentment, even in his agony. I do not understand. I feel anger, frustration, and sorrow; but these emotions mingle and fight for supremacy. Before Pilate, he was clearly of equal intellect, if not in command of the situation, though he ought to have been cowed. Is this the courage obtained through selfless acceptance of God's will? Perhaps it is not as simple as that. For a time, Pilate struggled with the situation until he acquiesced to the wishes of the baying crowds; and that awful sound still rings in my ears.

There are fewer people here on this grim place of death away from the comfort of the city: Mary, anguished, and some friends; a Temple representative to be able later to report a job nicely carried out by the Romans; of course, much soldiery, and a few "official" mourners so infuriating and upsetting to the genuine ones.

The Pharisees have had the last laugh now, or have they? This, after all, is what the Master predicted, though it is not at all clear to me in this haze of horror why this should be. I am not permitted to approach, and neither is Mary, his own mother. The shaft of a spear horizontally held has just told us as much. Now begins the horrifying ritual: the meticulous work of crucifixion. What words of encouragement can I shout? I cannot believe his stomach is not churning in anticipation of the pain to come, while his already broken body must be crying out in agony. I doubt I can shout at all. The Master has collapsed to the ground. The man who helped with his cross is being released from duty. The two thieves who are to be the Master's companions to the end are also on the ground, writhing. Their crosses are also being prepared. They curse and swear and make even more difficulties for themselves. A soldier kicks them. Oh, yes, how brave should I be? The onlookers' pain will disappear and the onlookers will shed no blood. The Master sits, head in hands at first, then he slowly raises his head. He knows what further pain awaits him: the thorny crown they put on his head lends nobility, not mockery. The sight recalls for me his words about practicing genuine piety. (Thinking about other things this way helps me distance myself from the scene before me and escape the awful emptiness of this waiting—as empty as the hungry-faced Pharisees, fasting so faithfully.) It is easy, the Master has told us, to fool men into thinking something about you, but you cannot fool God. You will not impress the Father simply by what men believe about you. You can impress men with your large, noisy coins dropping into the collection box. You can even give the impression that you are filling the collection box when you employ your skillful and practiced sleight of hand. Either way, you are intent upon impressing man rather than serving God.

Is he to die for telling a few simple truths?

Psalm 130

Out of the depths I cry to you, O Lord.

Reflection

Ash Wednesday is a day of fasting at the beginning of a season of fasting. At the beginning of his ministry, Jesus withdrew into the desert for a period of prayer and fasting. Fasting is a spiritual discipline through which people are prepared for the service of God and the struggle with evil.

Fasting is not an end in itself, but a way by which we offer up to God things—good in themselves—which can in the end enslave us if they are put in place of God. In that offering we are made free to know and to rejoice in the reality of God's love.

For further consideration…

How far do certain hypocritical actions displayed in today's Gospel parallel our own?

Thursday

Lamentations 1:3–4

Judah has gone into exile with suffering and hard servitude; she lives now among the nations, and finds no resting-place; her pursuers have all overtaken her in the midst of her distress.

The roads to Zion mourn, for no one comes to the festivals; all her gates are desolate, her priests groan; her young girls grieve, and her lot is bitter.

The Beloved Disciple:

I am now less collected but compulsively watching—watching, fascinated. My Lord is made to lie flat on the cross. A soldier orders the craftsman to begin his grisly work. But he thinks only of the work and gives meticulous attention to the preparation as he positions the arms, the hands, the legs, and the feet with an unnerving, almost clinical, precision. The thieves cry out and swear again and resist, only to be again bruised into submission. My Lord submits without resistance to the inevitable. I do nothing; I am doing nothing; I *can* do nothing. I am watching, watching as Jesus' arms are positioned again. He is embracing the world already, even before the nails secure this embrace.

I am trying to recite the prayer he taught us. It sticks on my tongue. The anticipation of the physical suffering is excruciating, and yet I cannot help but be mesmerized by the scene. Now, the craftsman stands back to admire his preparation or to assess the weight of my Master—probably the latter. Does he need to position a saddle on the cross to prevent the tearing away of the body once the cross is hoisted up? The man probably isn't heavy enough, the craftsman is thinking—but he looks as though he is marking the side of the cross. Perhaps he has decided to make sure. How this sickens me! Mary, in an agony of a different kind, stands here beside me, weeping and covering her eyes. I am almost suffocated by Mary's sorrow and my sorrow, and try to concentrate on other things. Yet I am rooted here, almost transfixed. This is true horror: waiting for even worse, knowing that it will come. The Master is already suffering much physical pain and sorrow, but now he smiles—albeit a difficult smile—in comfort, in the direction of his mother who does not see.

I am sure that the Master feels alone even among these clumps of people with different motives for their presence. It was alone and as a solitary figure that he faced the temptations in the wilderness, where his mission was finally forged in the barrenness of the desert. He had to seek his Father's will; in seeking it, the knowledge of it was made secure, the vocation clear. His course was obvious to him as soon as the obstacles were identified and other directions discarded and rejected.

Was it the Father's will that he should feed the hungry? Yes, in a sense, but he was setting us all up for heaven, not for a comfortable existence on earth. It was *our* duty as it was everyone's duty to feed the hungry, to console the dying, and to visit the sick and imprisoned. That was the natural pattern of a good life centered upon loving one's neighbor. Could he have brought everyone to the Father with even more spectacular miracles? Probably not, but can *this* really be his Father's will?

The feeding of the crowds—the five thousand or so—was that not an attempt at a humanitarian ministry? But no, I think that I realize now: it was significant as a parable concerned with sharing *him* as much as food. I don't know. These thoughts let me escape only momentarily.

Psalm 130

> *Lord, hear my voice! Let your ears be attentive to the voice of my supplications!*

Reflection

By quoting Scripture to the devil—"It is written, 'One does not live by bread alone but by every word that comes from the mouth of God'" (cf. Lk 4:4)—Jesus does not deny our real hunger, but points to God as the one who alone supplies our need. In St. John's Gospel, Jesus speaks of himself as the living bread, which comes down from heaven as the bread of life. God thereby supplies our need. "Whoever believes in me shall not hunger, and whoever believes in me shall never thirst."

For further consideration…

Do we take our Lord's words seriously? He is the "bread of life" and also "the way, the truth, and the life."

Friday

Lamentations 1:5–6

*Her foes have become the masters, her enemies prosper, because the L<small>ORD</small> has made her suffer for the multitude of her transgressions; her children have gone away, captives before the foe.
From daughter Zion has departed all her majesty.
Her princes have become like stags that find no pasture; they fled without strength before the pursuer.*

The Beloved Disciple:

And here I remain watching, impassive, not intervening, frightened to remain, fearful to leave. Mary is too distraught to be comforted by a reassuring hand, and my hand would reassure no one right now. My throat is tight with apprehension. Am I reassured by what is before me? Should this not reassure me, especially knowing that he predicted this and much greater things? Do I understand what he did predict? He predicted our despair, sure enough.

In the desert he was tempted by the spectacular. He could certainly have achieved a spectacular ministry, because he had absolute confidence that if he had chosen that way, he would have been protected by the angels of God, just as they have protected him in the way he did choose, which is the scene before me. Even so, his ministry has been spectacular at times, but never spectacular for its own sake.

Over there, is a beggar, one of the many odd characters who would attach themselves and who would always seem to recognize him as the Son of God. Do they now? The beggars wanted food and money (some were lazy!), but they did not expect those things of Jesus—others took care of that in his wake. That is what happened with the feeding of the crowds—spectacle was often the effect rather than the cause of his following. It was genuine modesty that appealed to him; he rejected the arrogant gesture.

And lying there, his cross being marked here and there for further work, he is the epitome of modesty and selflessness. The craftsman is marking the position of the Master's feet so that he can fix the foot rest with precision. The saddle and the foot rest will, in turn, determine the angle of the arms as they stretch up to the cross-beam. That angle will largely determine how soon the condemned man will die. If the poor creature is able to push up on his foot rest to aid his breathing for too long, or if for some reason the bodies are not permitted to remain hanging there, soldiers will break the legs, sometimes with cruel enjoyment.

Psalm 130

> *If you, O Lord, should mark iniquities, Lord, who could stand?*

Reflection

In the wilderness, the devil tempts Jesus to perform the spectacular, and even quotes Scripture to him.

The reply is short and to the point. Throughout the Gospels people come seeking a sign from Jesus and asking for a miracle, but miracles are ambiguous. Jesus does work miracles, but he is also very cautious about them. People seek a sign, but a sign is only given in response to faith, not to provide proof of who Jesus is.

For further consideration…

> It is good to remember that the devil is not shy of quoting Scripture.

Saturday

Lamentations 1:7–8

Jerusalem remembers, in the days of her affliction and wandering, all the precious things that were hers in days of old. When her people fell into the hand of the foe, and there was no one to help her, the foe looked on mocking over her downfall.

Jerusalem sinned grievously, so she has become a mockery; all who honoured her despise her, for they have seen her nakedness; she herself groans, and turns her face away.

The Beloved Disciple:

He told us that in the desert he was tempted to use his mission as the Zealots would have had him use it—with command of an army, a country, an empire, the world itself. He does not now seem to command anything but respect for his dignity in his indignity. His teaching suggested that the world had to be won for God through the heart, not by the sword.

Mary has just taken a few steps forward only to be thrust back, away from her recumbent son. The soldiers wish to avoid any interference with the smooth running of the operation. I now clutch Mary's shoulder, both in comfort and in order to discourage any impulsive move.

The craftsman is a wizened man in a leather apron: I have seen him about the city carrying a bag of the unpleasant tools of his trade. But his hammer is innocent enough; his nails blameless, though both will soon become cruel. He is making his way toward that bag of his. He kicks it open and, as he bends down, he nods to the senior soldier. The Master is pulled off the cross and to his feet and told to strip. He is now helped by two soldiers, not out of kindness but to assist in his humiliation. In the struggle with his clothes, the thorny crown is pulled off. As he stands in loin cloth only, his crown is roughly replaced with a sarcastic: "There you are, Your Majesty." The Master sways and collapses to his haunches and slumps backward. The clothes are placed in a pile, ready for the greedy soldiers—the perks of the crucifixion work unit. For a moment Mary holds out a hand in the belief, I think, that the clothes might be handed to her. She now withdraws her hand, knowing that that is not to be.

I have convinced myself that I am watching a drama in which I have no part and in which no part of me has any interest whatsoever. I know that this detachment will not last much longer. My great fear is that I will pluck up what I take to be courage and flee.

Now the craftsman selects a saddle block and a foot block from the pile not far from me. He looks at me in a matter-of-fact way, seemingly indifferent to what is unfolding. In doing so, though, he firmly draws me into his gruesome and evil world. Why should I resist? The Master is at this very moment the center of it.

Psalm 130

But there is forgiveness with you, so that you may be revered.

Reflection

Jesus is offered all the kingdoms of the world by the devil, but at a price; and the price is surrender to the fallen world and the power of evil. The devil claims possession of the world, but of course the world is God's, although it is fallen and under the influence of evil. The lie that the world belongs to the power of evil and not to God is paralleled by the invitation to Jesus to bow down and worship the devil. Jesus counters with the clear statement that worship belongs to God alone. What and who is ultimate? Who is worthy of worship? Is it the power of evil or God the Creator?

FOR FURTHER CONSIDERATION...

> How far does our behavior toward others help support the assertion that the world is under the influence of evil?

Lent I
Colt
Switch
Branch

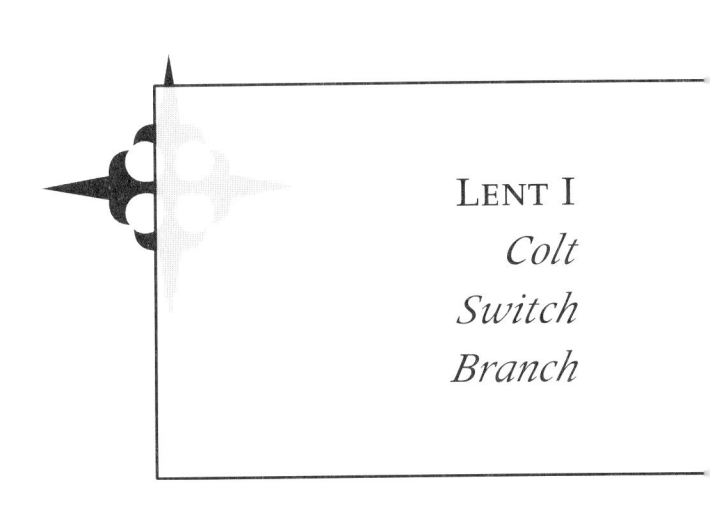

Monday 1

Lamentations 1:9

Her uncleanness was in her skirts; she took no thought of her future; her downfall was appalling, with none to comfort her. "O Lord, look at my affliction, for the enemy has triumphed!"

A Temple Official:

This really is most satisfactory—a happy ending indeed.

For so long we have wondered what would be the best thing to do. A number of times the Temple guards had been about to arrest him on some pretext or other, but always failed. It was just as well; the people probably would have rioted. They were fanatical. But he was an infernal nuisance, disturbing the tranquility of the cities, villages, and towns. Much of his preaching was blasphemous at worst, and, at best, highly disrespectful to those who so avidly carry out the will of the law. For blasphemy we were prepared to stone him—that would have been an end to him, all right. But, again, the people…. Many times we tried to entrap him to this end. Clever, I'll give him that.

There he is now, soon to be nailed down once and for all and out of our hair forever. He spoke lightly of his own religion, the faith of our father Abraham, but it was convenient to convert his blasphemy to treason and so win the justice of Rome.

What presumption—most fortunate for us—encouraging the crowds to blaspheme and hail him king when he came into Jerusalem the other day, stupidly sitting on that equally stupid animal, looking the fool he is.

Psalm 130

> *I wait for the Lord, my soul waits,*
> *and in his word I hope.*

Reflection

Jesus' journey to Jerusalem, his coming to the Holy City, is seen as more than just the journey of any Galilean countryman to the big city; it is even more than the pilgrim coming to worship and offer sacrifice at the temple. It is a new exodus, a journey of deliverance and of salvation. St. John's Gospel sees it as the journey of the Son to the Father—a journey that is made by the Son's perfect response to his Father's will.

FOR FURTHER CONSIDERATION...

With resolution our Lord set his face toward Jerusalem and all that that would mean. How easy is it for us to praise with our tongues one moment, and to curse the next?

Tuesday 1

Lamentations 1:10

*Enemies have stretched out their hands
over all her precious things; she has even seen
the nations invade her sanctuary, those whom
you forbade to enter your congregation.*

The Beloved Disciple:

And now the saddle and foot rest will be secured. But there will be no rest until he breathes his last. I am trying to avoid watching Jesus. In contrast, his mother now stares at him in tearful disbelief at what we are witnessing.

The craftsman is kneeling beside the trunk of the cross and sits the saddle upon it, lining it up with the marks drawn on the side. One heavy blow from the hammer wielded by this deceptively slight but strong individual will fix the foot-long split nail into the wood; a second, and the nail will penetrate the saddle and pierce the main beam; a third, and the nail will be home.

The split ends will be bent their separate ways after the cross has been hoisted high on the hill.

Mary and I are permitted quiet words of comfort, but they would be drowned among the cries and curses of the two to be crucified with Jesus. What quiet words of comfort can you give? I can think of none even if I could articulate any. The mostly fickle crowds have dissolved, there are a few of us standing silent on this hillside. A contrast indeed with the adulation with which he was received astride the donkey. This deeply significant gesture, as I thought at the time, now has no meaning at all.

Psalm 130

My soul waits for the LORD more than those who watch for the morning, more than those who watch for the morning.

Reflection

Some of the Pharisees had heard the cries: "Blessed is the King who comes in the name of the Lord! Peace in heaven and glory in the highest!" It was very dangerous; not at all orthodox. And they had protested about it. And so the scene was set.

FOR FURTHER CONSIDERATION...

Perhaps we might compare the cry of the crowds: "Peace in heaven and glory in the highest!" with the angel's cry of "Glory to God in the highest, and on earth peace among those whom he favors...!"

Wednesday 1

Lamentations 1:11

All her people groan as they search for bread; they trade their treasures for food to revive their strength. Look, O L<small>ORD</small>, and see how worthless I have become.

The Beloved Disciple:

Yes, the crowds were full of enthusiasm and excitement on that day. Many in those crowds heard his trial: some sidled off; others cried out for Barabbas and for the blood of Jesus simply because of the prompting of the chief priests and the elders. Most deserted him as he knew would happen. Even of the twelve, few remained, and fewer remain anywhere near now. I am here not through courage. I long to run away and hide. I cannot count myself anyone's superior for my presence here.

The children always knew. "Become like these," he would say, "because their instincts have not been blunted either by superstition or sophistication. They may not have years of learning, but their perception is sharp." But *what* did the children know?

The wiry old craftsman is picking up his hammer, long familiar to his hand, and the action urges me out of reverie. Three hammer blows snap mockingly at me with pent-up aggression. "Colt! Switch! Branch!" they seem to say. The saddle on the cross is fixed.

Psalm 130

> *O Israel, hope in the Lord! For with the Lord there is steadfast love, and with him is great power to redeem.*

Reflection

The prophets of Israel were often uncomfortable people. They were disturbers, prickers of the balloon of complacency. Jeremiah inveighs against those who parrot the cry, "The Temple of the Lord, the Temple of the Lord," believing themselves inviolable. Jeremiah is commanded by God to stand outside the gate of the Temple and proclaim: "The Lord, the God of Israel, says this: 'Amend your behavior and your actions and I will stay with you in this place…but steal, would you, murder, commit adultery, perjure yourselves…follow alien gods? You do all this and then present yourselves in the

Temple, saying "now we are safe." Do you take this Temple that bears my name for a robbers' den? I am not blind.'"

Jesus enters the Temple and drives out the traders and the sellers of sacrificial animals; the words of Jeremiah rise to his lips: "...but you make it a den of robbers."

What really brought about Jesus' crucifixion? Much of it was Jesus' words and deeds about the Temple.

For further consideration...

> Our Lord said that we must become as children. A monastic principle states: "Feel compunction rather than know the meaning of the word."

Thursday 1

Lamentations 1:12

Is it nothing to you, all you who pass by?
Look and see if there is any sorrow like my sorrow,
*which was brought upon me, which the L*ord
inflicted on the day of his fierce anger.

The Beloved Disciple:

Those mocking sounds warn of more vicious sounds to come. The inevitability of his crucifixion now is hammered home. Mary is clutching my arm as the craftsman moves to work on the other two crosses.

There is a little commotion. More Temple officials are arriving, arguing, it seems, with a centurion. I cannot hear, but I still hear the words of the hammer. I see again the colt trotting dutifully beside my Master mounted on the ass; I see the switches torn from the trees by the people lauding their great teacher, come from God; I see again the branches torn down and spread before him to honor him on his way. I see the switch he used to drive out the deceivers and defrauders from the Temple court. I hear him weep over the Temple and over Jerusalem for the inhabitants' lack of faith and lack of preparation for their own souls, despite all the prophets' warnings. I envisage the switches and branches surely used to scourge the Master before his journey here to Golgotha.

Psalm 130

It is he who will redeem Israel from all its iniquities.

Reflection

As Jesus comes to the crest of the Mount of Olives and sees Jerusalem, he breaks into tears. The city of peace has not known and lived by the things that belong to its peace or embodied its peace. And so judgment will come. There will not be one stone left standing on another. And so, Jesus weeps over Jerusalem; weeps over the city of peace, which has been blind to what peace is. The new Jerusalem embodies, in the power of the Resurrection, the things that belong to peace.

For further consideration…

We are already made new in Christ. In what ways do we make this truth apparent?

Friday 1

Lamentations 1:13

From on high he sent fire; it went deep into my bones; he spread a net for my feet; he turned me back; he has left me stunned, faint all day long.

The Beloved Disciple:

The waiting and the watching are difficult to bear. The soldiers are deciding who should own my Master's clothes. There is much carefree fun and joviality. It is no concern of theirs that a grave miscarriage of justice is about to occur; they have seen it all before. Jesus waits.

Many in the crowd who greeted him with palms and olive branches were there because of the risen Lazarus, the brother of Martha and Mary. Jesus is fond of the whole family and it was for them that this extraordinary miracle was performed. Jairus' daughter he brought back to life, and that widow's son, I remember, but they were essentially domestic affairs. The raising up of Lazarus was more remarkable because it was public and seemed pregnant with meaning, as though it were one of his parables. But that meaning is too well hidden.

It is disturbing to think of these things as the Master is being so carefully prepared for death.

Psalm 22

> *My God, my God, why have you forsaken me?*
> *Why are you so far from helping me, from the*
> *words of my groaning?*

Reflection

Pilgrims trudging up the hill to Jerusalem for the feast of the Passover would have been stirred by the knot of Galileans around a man on a donkey. People were shouting and cheering, waving branches of palm and olive. They were cheering the man on the donkey—a very ordinary sight in itself—as though he were a king, throwing their cloaks before him as a sign of homage. A few might have thought of the prophecy of Zechariah about God's anointed one coming to the Holy City without any sign or rank of splendor. What might this mean, this symbolic coming of Jesus to Jerusalem at the time of the feast of deliverance, the celebration of the freeing of the people of Israel from slavery in Egypt?

FOR FURTHER CONSIDERATION...

> Lazarus was brought back to life; he would die again. Christ rose from the dead to die no more; death would have no more dominion over him.

Saturday 1

Lamentations 1:14

My transgressions were bound into a yoke; by his hand they were fastened together; they weigh on my neck, sapping my strength; the L<small>ORD</small> handed me over to those whom I cannot withstand.

The Beloved Disciple:

The methodical craftsman is returning to the cross in front of me. His matter-of-factness is frightening: he would have the same attitude and demeanor if he were repairing the door of my home.

The recently arrived officials from the Temple are most heated in their argument with the centurion. He is holding what looks like an indictment plaque. I am ashamed to feel grateful for the diversion as I stand and wait with Mary.

I can now see others only just familiar to me by sight, and some close followers of Jesus, appearing at various distances from this point—little clutches of deep sorrow and huddles of despair. Greater numbers are watching the fate of the other prisoners. Mary and I will be permitted to converse with Jesus once this ghastly preparation is over and the final stage reached. The death of the Christ is contrary to what I have understood. He was unwavering in asserting his special relationship to God the almighty Father, so I cannot doubt that he is the Christ. Yet how can this suffering and death be part of God's plan? What else, though, could his vineyard story foretell?

Psalm 22

> *O my God, I cry by day, but you do not answer; and by night, but find no rest.*

Reflection

What had been proclaimed in Galilee must also be proclaimed in Jerusalem, at the very center of the faith of Israel. Jesus rides into Jerusalem; the crowds cheer; and then? Some great intervention by God? No, but an attack on the Temple traders, and an assertion about the nature of worship. No great popular rising; no expulsion of the Roman power; only, for the rest of his days in Jerusalem, the steady, inexorable, closing in of the hostile powers.

FOR FURTHER CONSIDERATION...

When the hostile powers close in on the heir to the vineyard, they will kill the heir. The paradox is that the heir is also the vine itself, and God the Father the vinedresser.

LENT II
Take
Break
Feed

Monday 2

Lamentations 2:8

*The Lord determined to lay in ruins the wall
of daughter Zion; he stretched the line; he did not
withhold his hand from destroying; he caused rampart
and wall to lament; they languish together.*

Simon Peter:

What weakness! What shame! "I am a worm," as the psalmist says, "and no man." It was I who pronounced him the Christ; I who saw it and said so.

"Curb your exuberance," he has said on many occasions, gently, if I became excited at the prospect of a fresh project, a new mission. Now he prepares to die as I skulk, mortified. It all began to fall apart for me in that upper room we rented. First, I would not have my feet washed, then I changed my mind: "Wash my head and my hands as well!" I said. I felt stupid when Jesus told me that it wasn't necessary. Waves of shame alternating with self-pity wash over me now. "I'll go to the ends of the earth for you!" I afterward declared. "You'll deny me, Peter, three times before the cock crows." How crushing was that condemnation! I couldn't understand these words. Why should Jesus turn on me in that way; and, being forewarned, why could I not summon the strength to resist the coward's way? I was too ashamed to admit my association with him to a mere girl, who, after all, was only making a sensible observation. Three times I denied knowing Jesus, whom *I* identified as the Christ. Never before has a morning alarm awakened me to the horror of my weaknesses. Oh, that *look...*

Psalm 22

> *Yet you are holy, enthroned on the praises*
> *of Israel.*

Reflection

What is certain is that the context of Jesus' dying was Passover; and Passover was concerned with God's mighty acts, concerned with a deliverance from slavery and a remembrance of such a deliverance. The Passover was a memorial of deliverance from Egypt. In making and keeping this memorial, time was telescoped.

Bitter herbs were chewed so that the tasting of bitterness linked the present with the past.

For further consideration...

Our "Peterness" is very apparent. We can prepare the upper room in the morning and deny Christ in the evening.

Tuesday 2

Lamentations 2:9

*Her gates have sunk into the ground; he has ruined and broken her bars; her king and princes are among the nations; guidance is no more, and her prophets obtain no vision from the L*ORD.

The Beloved Disciple:

My arm surrounds Mary's shoulders. They shudder involuntarily now and again. We are both watching the craftsman in the foreground, perhaps as intently as a pair of apprentices watch their employer for fear of being asked searching questions that they find themselves unable to answer. In the background is Jesus, naked except for a loin cloth, seemingly studying the same scene from a rather different perspective. Can he detach himself from reality and remember the tools he knew so well in his father's workshop? The calculated monotony of this lingering prelude is unbearable.

The foot block or rest has been selected—I believe it is also called a "shoe," and there's some irony in that. In placing it on the main beam, the craftsman lines it up with the mark he has made. He now picks up one of his formidable nails—its brothers will have to perform the more bloody duties—and stands it on the block. The resounding blows quite distinctly say: "Take! Break! Feed!" and the block is secure.

Why do those words snap at me now; those words so gently spoken? Perhaps because this violence about to erupt before me must first occur in order to make sense of his words. But what sense will it make? What sense can it make? "Take! Break! Feed!"

Psalm 22

In you our ancestors trusted; they trusted,
and you delivered them.

Reflection

What is new in Jesus' action is not the taking of bread and giving thanks over it, but the identification of it with his body. Jesus, the host, takes bread—bread which is life and the most ordinary of things, the food we need in order to live. This very bread is my body, he says. In the Old Testament not only words but actions are prophetic. A cloak is torn, and a kingdom is divided. Prophets speak by signs, and these signs are seen as somehow triggering an action that follows from them. Jesus takes bread and breaks it, and identifies it with himself. Already in the upper room, the movement of his self-offering is begun.

For further consideration...

The sound of the breaking of the host on the altar also causes the telescoping of time. However, this food is given for our sustenance now.

Wednesday 2

Lamentations 2:10

The elders of daughter Zion sit on the ground in silence; they have thrown dust on their heads and put on sackcloth; the young girls of Jerusalem have bowed their heads to the ground.

The Beloved Disciple:

The Master's body is soon to be broken on the cross just like the bread that he broke before us and called his body, but my mind can take this proposition no further. In a way, that meal had every feature and sign of being our final act together—a farewell from the Master. How could that black-hearted companion of ours precipitate this disaster?

The shoes are about to be fitted on the thieves' crosses; the thieves are a little quieter. They, like the Master, are undressed. They stole; their clothes are taken and their lives will be taken. If there is justice in their case, there is none in my Master's.

The heated discussion between the Temple officials and the centurion is subsiding; the centurion is patting the plaque and shrugging his shoulder, perhaps in sympathy with their point of view.

Difficult also to grasp were the Master's subsequent words. The wine cup was to be as his blood, he said, poured out for all. This feels so much like a dream that I am sure I can walk over to him, brushing through the fence of horizontal spears, and question him about the meaning of these things. The wisdom of not doing so is clear to me: the weapons are real, the soldiers are real, the drama no dream, the drama not make-believe.

Psalm 22

To you they cried, and were saved; in you they trusted, and were not put to shame.

Reflection

The bread that is broken is the bread of which Jesus said, "This is my body." The sign of broken bread points inexorably to the broken body and the pouring out of his blood. "Breaking" is the language of sacrifice and sacrifice is at the heart of what was done on Calvary. At its heart it is an offering and an immolation for the establishment or renewal of communion. What begins in the earlier strands of the Old Testament as the offering of lambs, or the blood of bulls and goats, moves on, through the psalmist's "the sacrifice of God is...a broken and contrite heart...," to an offering in which we now can personally participate.

For further consideration...

> The outpouring of the chalice of consecrated wine is the generous spilling of the life-giving blood of the Church, as the outpouring of wine from the water pitchers in Cana is a foretaste of this Passion, established at the beginning of our Lord's ministry.

Thursday 2

Lamentations 2:11

My eyes are spent with weeping; my stomach churns; my bile is poured out on the ground because of the destruction of my people, because infants and babes faint in the streets of the city.

The Beloved Disciple:

More people are arriving; they are keeping their distance. Mary and I are here close to what is happening. We can move no closer. We were together at Cana when Jesus said to his mother with a smile: "What am I to do? I had not intended to begin my mission on this day, in this place!" He acquiesced to her entreaty and helped recover the reputation of the host. So many of his miracles were also parables: he taught us through them. And now I suddenly see that this so very domestic miracle at the beginning of his ministry showed us the outpouring of his blood on this day, an outpouring we shall soon witness.

This revelation has helped me little. Memories are rushing headlong into my mind, uncontrolled. How perverse! I am compelled to concentrate on what is happening about me in this place.

The saddles and shoes of the thieves' crosses are fixed, and the indictment plaques are now being nailed. The centurion is handing another to the craftsman: I believe it to be the Master's. What does it say? Treason? Blasphemy?

If either, his words were obviously never heard.

Psalm 22

> *But I am a worm and not human; scorned by others, and despised by the people.*

Reflection

The breaking of the Lord's body on the cross was preceded by another breaking, a breaking of communion by betrayal. Our Lord's sacrifice was born of the darkness of betrayal and abandonment. With the cross he bears the weight of sin, the weight of betrayal, the weight of the denial of communion.

For further consideration…

As the host is broken upon the altar as a prelude to Communion, how often has our betrayal of his Word broken that very Communion?

Friday 2

Lamentations 2:12

*They cry to their mothers, "Where is bread and wine?"
as they faint like the wounded in the streets of the city,
as their life is poured out on their mothers' bosom.*

The Beloved Disciple:

Jesus told me who he knew would betray him to the chief priests. I hear that Judas, in remorse, has killed himself. "This is the man, the man I am greeting. This is he." What did he hope to gain? Possibly a little money? But many liars and perjurers were found or paid in order to enable the chief priests to take Jesus before Pilate. If the Romans kill him, the chief priests will not be blamed by the people. Judas, then, merely identified Jesus in the darkness—the first step in the chief priests' plan to be rid of the Christ because he did not fit their preconception of the Savior. He frightened them.

But the sad sight before me now, wept over by his mother, will frighten few people. He now suffers extreme degradation and humiliation. Did he not explain all this to us? Could he have meant condemnation as a state criminal and death in this way? This does not fit my preconception of the Christ either.

The craftsman is reading the plaque he has been given. He looks surprised and looks up at the centurion, who once more shrugs his shoulders and turns the palms of his hands upward in a gesture of mock hopelessness.

Psalm 22

*All who see me mock at me;
they make mouths at me.*

Reflection

At supper, Jesus lets Judas go. The betrayer is free to choose what to do and how to act. Judas shows his failure to recognize the demands of love by choosing the darkness rather than the light.

For further consideration...

Our betrayals are often more subtle than Judas.' They are often difficult to detect as we keep them even from ourselves.

Saturday 2

Lamentations 2:13

*What can I say for you, to what compare you,
O daughter Jerusalem? To what can I likened you, that
I may comfort you, O virgin daughter Zion? For vast
as the sea is your ruin; who can heal you?*

The Beloved Disciple:

Jesus told Peter that he could not follow him now, but that he would do so later. Is *this* his route back to the Father? What of us now? Shall we fish again and, in time, put aside these years in our minds as nothing more than an interesting interlude? I cannot believe that it is all to no avail. For Jesus, each event has always seemed a step forward, whether a modest triumph or an acrimonious rejection.

I think I can see the other Marys and Salome keeping to themselves at a distance. It would be of comfort to me and to his mother if they were to join us, because worse is to come and Mary's despair will deepen further as the hours die.

Psalm 22

> *They shake their heads; "Commit your cause*
> *to the Lord; let him deliver—let him rescue*
> *the one in whom he delights!"*

Reflection

The betrayer has left the supper room. Judas will identify Jesus; Peter will deny Jesus.

The problem of keeping the commandments, as St. Paul found and argues in his letter to the Romans, is that commands are double-edged. We fail, and the law we believed we could obey, and which we strove to follow, stands in judgment over our failure. However, Paul made the overwhelming discovery that God had already accepted him in love by the very act of sending his Son into the world.

For further consideration…

> Despite our betrayals and denials we are accepted in love by God.

Lent III
*Sweat
Blood
Kiss*

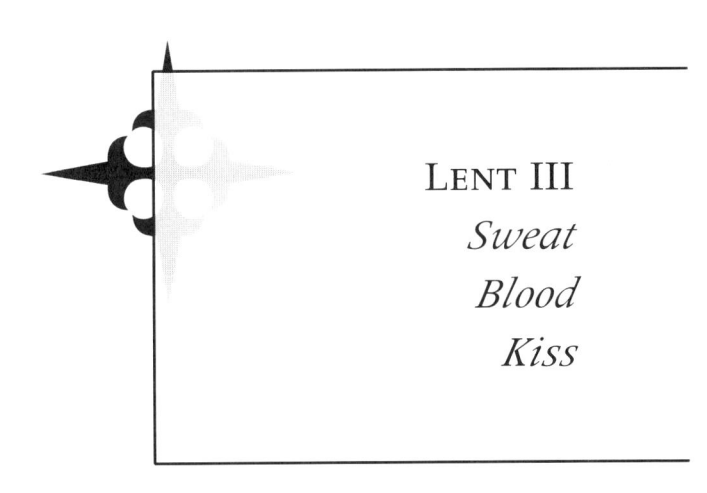

Monday 3

Lamentations 2:14

Your prophets have seen for you false and deceptive visions; they have not exposed your iniquity to restore your fortunes, but have seen oracles for you that are false and misleading.

Mary, the Mother of Jesus:

Heavenly Father, you are about to take away the Son you gave me all those years ago. Your messenger told me that his name would be great and that he would be the one spoken of by the prophets of old. With Joseph, I found a place in Bethlehem and there I nursed him. The common folk came from the hilltop, and illustrious ones knelt before him. We named him and presented him to you. Through Simeon you told me of momentous things that would occur because of him, and that I should suffer in my duties to you. These warnings have come horribly to pass. Forgive me. Hold him in your arms until he commends his spirit to you. Give me strength and steadfastness, perseverance and resolution to remain here, faithful to my Son and your Son, until and beyond the time you take him to continue to do your will. I believe but do not understand. Strengthen me also to be able to do what you would have me do. Thank you, O Heavenly Father, for the gift of your Son, of my Son; for the work he has done and for the work he will do.

Psalm 22

Yet it was you who took me from the womb;
you kept me safe on my mother's breast.

Reflection

Jesus existed as one of us, in our situation, living as man toward death, living as man with the possibility of God. In his life the power and presence of God were so manifest that in encountering him, men and women were made whole, knew themselves judged, and knew themselves forgiven. "Lord, to whom else shall we go?" said Peter. "You have the words of eternal life."

For further consideration...

If we are open about our weaknesses and sin to the God of Love, we then know forgiveness.

Tuesday 3

Lamentations 2:15

All who pass along the way clap their hands at you; they hiss and wag their heads at daughter Jerusalem; "Is this the city that was called the perfection of beauty, the joy of all the earth?"

The Beloved Disciple:

Soon the cross will be hauled to a position where it can be hoisted into its shuttered slot in the ground. But first, the indictment plaque will be fixed. The order of these things is meticulous and well-rehearsed.

A smaller nail has been selected and, at what will be the uppermost part of the cross, the wizened man is now kneeling with hammer held. Three hammer blows secure the plaque, and again, three single syllables now assail my ears. The last seems to hiss as the hammer—its job done—ricochets off the plaque. "Sweat! Blood! Kiss!"

I am looking at Jesus slumped on the ground, waiting to be taken to the cross and fixed to it. I cannot see the indictment from this angle. I can see a rivulet of startlingly red blood from the point of a thorn in the middle of his forehead making its way down his nose. That was the path taken by great drops of sweat in Gethsemane as Jesus, deep in prayer, wrestled with what he knew was to come.

Psalm 22

On you I was cast from my birth, and since my mother bore me you have been my God.

Reflection

"You have the words of eternal life," said Peter. And yet Jesus, so powerfully attractive and at the same time so challenging, spoke of the necessity for us to find that true life through a dying. It is the one who is willing to lose his or her life who will find it, whereas the person who takes care to save his or her life will lose it. Jesus' disciples must take up their cross and follow him. They are to be baptized with the baptism that he is baptized with and drink the same cup— that cup which Jesus in agony, grappling with the dust of Gethsemane and sweating blood, longed to pass from him.

For further consideration...

If we let our cross drop, it will fall again across the shoulders of Christ himself.

Wednesday 3

Lamentations 3:1–3

*I am one who has seen affliction under the rod
of God's wrath; he has driven and brought me
into darkness without any light; against me alone he
turns his hand, again and again, all day long.*

The Beloved Disciple:

In Gethsemane his head glistened as though anointed with the oil produced by the presses there. We all believed him chosen, anointed for God's purposes. The scene before me now is despair and defeat, but the Master's attitude there in the garden was of one reaching the final stages of his life's work, painful and grueling though it was going to be. His followers certainly did not support him in this belief. Slowly they fell away during the succeeding events. In the garden vigil we could scarcely keep our eyes open. We did not grasp the importance or the significance of the occasion. He knew, of course. But the evidence of this scene before me looks little like victory and achievement. God, our Father in heaven, give me understanding.

The craftsman is standing back from the crosses as they are dragged further over so that the bases will point to the underground scabbards that will hold them upright.

Psalm 22

> *Do not be far from me, for trouble is near and there is no one to help.*

Reflection

Jesus shows that there is a dying to be accomplished before coming to the moment of earthly death; a dying that is a daily dying to self, a dying to sin, to the placing of ourselves at the center of our universe.

For further consideration...

There are many things that militate against our fulfilling our vocations as "other Christs." Why doesn't Christ's love shine from my face?

Thursday 3

Lamentations 3:4–6

He has made my flesh and my skin to waste away, and broken my bones; he has besieged and enveloped me with bitterness and tribulation; he has made me sit in darkness like the dead of long ago.

The Beloved Disciple:

Judas appeared, in the company of thugs and agents of the chief priests and elders, to greet Jesus and to point him out to the mob. It was dark and there were few lanterns and torches. Even then, Jesus appeared master of the situation, saying, "There's no need for all this. I am here."

He now no longer appears master of the situation—unless all these people are doing what God requires of them. If this is so, it is beyond my comprehension. It is all too vile. Judas' kiss marked him out to die.

The Master is calm, knowing that he will soon be taken to the cross once more; but the thieves are not. The rising crescendo of swearing and cursing as they realize their time approaches accompanies the grunts of the soldiers as they draw the crosses along the ground to the places allotted.

Psalm 22

> *Many bulls encircle me, strong bulls of Bashan surround me.*

Reflection

Let us remind ourselves that the breaking of the Lord's body on the cross was preceded by another breaking, a breaking of communion by the darkness of betrayal. The kiss of Judas is part of the Passion of our Lord, the betrayal by "my own familiar friend whom I trusted, who has lifted up his hand against me."

For further consideration...

In pointing out the Master in the darkness, Judas is denying his association with him. "This is the man, all right: don't associate me with him, however." Are these ever our words?

Friday 3

Lamentations 3:7–9

He has walled me about so that I cannot escape; he has put heavy chains on me; though I call and cry for help, he shuts out my prayer; he has blocked my ways with hewn stones, he has made my paths crooked.

The Beloved Disciple:

There is a level "table" here on the top of the hill, so that any final adjustments can be made by the craftsman of the day, and the crosses completed for the work they will have to do. They are positioned correctly, ready for the fixing of the prisoners. In popular idiom they are then "launched." It appears that the Master will be flanked by the two miscreants.

Mary is bracing herself for the cruel wounding of her Son's hands and feet, which will test us all.

That Jesus healed the injured servant's ear passed almost unnoticed at his arrest. In fact, he facilitated his own arrest by quelling the scuffles that had broken out around him, thus making it easier for the officers of the Temple to apprehend him.

All three crosses are in position and the cross on the right will be occupied first. A soldier struggles with one of the thieves and lays him flat on the cross. Suddenly, the man is releasing a blood-curdling yell.

Psalm 22

> *They open wide their mouths at me,*
> *like a ravening and roaring lion.*

Reflection

The Passion of our Lord begins in the darkness of betrayal and abandonment.

For further consideration...

With the identifying kiss, Judas has set in motion a chain of events. His subsequent regret comes too late; the dye has been cast.

Saturday 3

Lamentations 3:22–24

The steadfast love of the Lord never ceases; his mercies never come to an end; they are new every morning; great is your faithfulness. "The Lord is my portion," says my soul, "therefore will I hope in him."

The Beloved Disciple:

The nails secure the thief. The Master is next. No, curiously, it has been decided to secure the other thief first and leave the central cross unoccupied for a few moments more. The other is being led over to his cross. He knows further resistance is useless. The nailing of these two fails to affect me or Mary except with a feeling of sympathy for their pain. This is merely a prelude: we are conserving our indignation.

The Master now looks up and across to his mother, then to me. He shakes his head slowly and holds up his right hand as if to say, "Keep calm, all is well." His head and hand drop to their former positions.

The craftsman looks pleased. Now he is selecting three more large-headed nails for much crueler work.

Psalm 22

I am poured out like water, and all my bones are out of joint; my heart is like wax, it is melted within my breast.

Reflection

The letter to the Hebrews speaks of Christ as the great High Priest. The end of Temple priesthood and the end of Temple sacrifice come together in the One who is both priest and victim, the offerer and the offered.

For further consideration...

Darkness is the cloak of sin. Christ illuminates the darkest recesses, that morning star who dispels the darkness and night.

Lent IV
Priest
King
Judge

Monday 4

Lamentations 3:25–30

The LORD is good to those who wait for him, to the soul that seeks him. It is good that one should wait quietly for the salvation of the LORD. It is good for one to bear the yoke in youth, to sit alone in silence when the LORD has imposed it, to put one's mouth to the dust (there may yet be hope), to give one's cheek to the smiter, and be filled with insults.

Pontius Pilate:

My wife sent a message during my examination of Jesus. "Have nothing to do with the condemnation of Jesus." Her intuition is always impeccable. However, when he was to be brought before me I was compelled to hear what the Jewish authorities had to say. I could not retort, "My wife is uneasy about all this, take the case elsewhere." I had to take the case.

I had heard about him, of course. Who hadn't? But what a man! He was not, though, what I expected; a philosopher, clearly, and a man with a vigorous mind, revealed, paradoxically, by his saying very little. "What is truth?" I asked, because the conversation, such as it was, was difficult for me. At first, I thought the question "What is truth?" to be a clever piece of rhetoric. Then it dawned on me that it wasn't. There is manifestly only one truth, but we make our own with borrowed facets of the real truth affixed, to beguile the opponent. There are Roman truths and Jewish truths. There are chief priests' truths; there is expedient truth; there is convenient truth; there is half-remembered truth, forgotten truth, and, finally, untruth.

I took note of my wife's cautionary words. When I discovered that the chief priests were determined that the man whom they feared should die, I told them I would wash my hands of the case. "Good," they said. "We are happy to have the responsibility."

Now as he waits on Golgotha it's immaterial to him who has washed his hands of his death or who is shouldering responsibility for it. After giving in to their demands—and for the sake of expediency it was prudent that I should do so—I was powerless to do any more except enjoy the satisfaction of giving instructions for his indictment plaque. What indeed is truth?

Psalm 22

> *My mouth is dried up like potsherd,*
> *and my tongue sticks to my jaws;*
> *you lay me in the dust of death.*

Reflection

The Jewish leaders had little liking for potential disturbers of the peace. Cruel reprisals were likely to follow if the Romans felt threatened. Not just one or two, but several hundred might be crucified to teach the others a lesson. So the high priest counsels that it is expedient that one man die for the people. What is more, Caiaphas would have the support of the Pharisees—and that was by no means always the case. These very careful religious men were known not to care for the teaching of Jesus—a dangerous radical.

For further consideration...

> How often do we think it expedient—politically correct and convenient, but not necessarily honest or just— for us to do or say what we do or say?

Tuesday 4

Lamentations 4:1

How the gold has grown dim, how the pure gold is changed! The sacred stones lie scattered at the head of every street.

The Beloved Disciple:

So desperately did the high priest examine him on the charge of blasphemy that the examination was a farce. Many times had the same accusations been leveled against him. It was enough to hear the accusation; that was sufficient.

Mary is clasping my hand tightly, and I am clasping hers. We try to summon courage and fortitude as the Master is led to succumb to the bloody work of the craftsman. The craftsman is long-skilled and trained in woodwork and metalwork; he has had to acquire skill to mix his materials further and add flesh to his repertoire. The Master does not need to be pulled or pushed. He is walking the few paces. He is lowering himself and positioning himself, to the genuine admiration of the centurion. My insides now feel twisted and torn as anticipation and apprehension seize me.

Mary has freed her hand and is burying her face in both her hands and falling to her knees.

Psalm 22

> *For dogs are all around me; a company of evildoers encircles me. My hands and my feet have shriveled.*

Reflection

Earlier, the Pharisees had advised Jesus on his entry into Jerusalem: "Teacher, tell them to shut up; you know that those slogans are not only potential dynamite, they are also unorthodox; if you allow it to go on you are implying that you are the chosen King, the Messiah, God's representative." And all that Jesus had said was that if he were to stop them from cheering, the stones would start shouting. He had shown he endorsed such ideas—a dangerous character indeed.

For further consideration...

> Jesus displays kingship and kingliness. May we reveal the nature of his kingdom in our very lives.

Wednesday 4

Lamentations 4:2

The precious children of Zion, worth their weight in fine gold—how they are reckoned as earthen pots, the work of a potter's hands!

The Beloved Disciple:

I now cannot turn away or hide my face. I am watching intently. A nail has been selected and is in the craftsman's hand, his hammer in the other. The left arm of Jesus has been positioned and he does not resist as the nail is rested on his hand. The soldier's knee is not required. Three hammer blows and the Master winces: "Priest! King! Judge!" The words rush at me more terrifyingly as I know they accompany searing pain.

The chief priests pressed the high priest. The chief priests were jealous of their position, the high priest of his. Somehow the charge of blasphemy had to be converted into treason. "Priest" whispers about my ears; "priest"—there to protect the sacred traditions, the law, the prophets, justice; "priest"—there to be a priest of God.

After the initial shock of the nail penetrating her Son's flesh, Mary is uncovering her face to allow its sorrow to stare at her Son.

Psalm 22

> *I can count all my bones.*
> *They stare and gloat over me.*

Reflection

The pain of Peter's denial must have been keen and terrible—Peter, who had been the first to confess his faith in Jesus as the Christ of God. Peter's assertion: "No, I don't know him, I really don't know him. I don't know what you are talking about. How could you think I had anything to do with that man, that one on the losing side, that one who might land me in jail too if I admit I know him? Jesus? No, I never knew him."

For further consideration…

When the cock began to crow, Peter felt regret. The crowing of the cock meant something to Peter only because of Jesus' prediction. The cock crow was indeed the morning alarm for Peter to come to his senses. May we be alert to such alarms.

Thursday 4

Lamentations 4:3

Even the jackals offer the breast and nurse their young, but my people have become cruel, like the ostriches in the wilderness.

The Beloved Disciple:

The other nails will be easier—for me, at least. To prolong the agony, the craftsman has been called to loop the ropes around the cross-beams of the other two crosses so that they can be "launched" on either side of the place reserved for the Master's cross. The Master lies gazing sadly upward, his left arm fixed now until death.

Kingship was their masterstroke. If he claimed kingship, then the Roman authorities must be made to take an interest. In their appeal to Pilate, the chief priests were adamant that he was a threat to Caesar. What would they care?

The other Marys and Salome have drawn nearer, and we have just exchanged glances, but no words. Mary's sister is coming toward us. She is extending an arm to clutch Mary's arm. She now returns to the others a few paces to our right.

Psalm 22

> *They divide my garments among themselves,*
> *and for my clothing they cast lots.*

Reflection

St. John sees the cross as the place of our Lord's glorification, the place where he is enthroned as a king.

For further consideration…

Truth will be apparent only after Pilate's equivocation, and Caiaphas' thoughts of expediency are nailed to the cross along with our sins.

Friday 4

Lamentations 4:4

The tongue of the infant sticks to the roof of its mouth for thirst; the children beg for food, but no one gives them anything

The Beloved Disciple:

Priest! King! Judge! still reverberate. All three words should suggest the comfort of justice and mercy. Now they simply mean corruption, perjury, and the slaughter of the innocent.

In a few hours my life has been turned on its head. The Master's teaching, his parables and his miracles relating to the Kingdom of Heaven, seem meaningless. But why should they? That the servant of God, the Son of Man, the Son of God the Father should suffer has been his constant theme and the theme of the prophets. Why should I now doubt? And yet, what can now possibly come to spell victory and triumph? Lazarus comes to mind, and the parable of the vineyard, but nothing really helps.

Mary is gazing at Jesus through large, sad, tear-filled eyes. And she stands again.

Psalm 22

> *But you, O Lord, do not be far away!*
> *O my help, come quickly to my aid!*

Reflection

St. John's account of the trial before Pilate is heavy with irony. It is supposed to be Jesus who is being tried, but it is Pilate, Herod, and the Jewish leaders who are actually on trial. Both by his silence and his comments, Jesus shows that he is the one who judges.

For further consideration...

Our actions and words judge us long before we reach trial.

Saturday 4

Lamentations 4:5

*Those who feasted on delicacies perish in the streets;
those who were brought up in purple cling to ash heaps.*

The Beloved Disciple:

The crosses of the thieves are successfully looped and their bases placed behind the shafts at the start of two, forty-five-degree slopes into the shafts. Two soldiers stand guard at the base of the right-hand cross and two soldiers hold the ropes. The centurion cries out and the cross rises creakingly and precariously upward, jolting violently as it finds its way into the shallow shaft. It sways slightly, still held by the soldiers. One of the soldiers at the foot of the cross drops the vast wooden block behind, and the cross is set. The operation has caused the unfortunate man to cry out in pain as his hands tear slightly, hands that have stolen, it is true. My Lord's hands will similarly suffer: his hands have blessed, healed, and broken bread.

Psalm 22

> *Deliver my soul from the sword,*
> *my life from the power of the dog!*

Reflection

Crucifixion was the most appalling death meted out to criminals—and the Jews regarded the one who suffered it as being beyond the reaches of even the fringes of the community of Israel. Yet from this death the glory of God is shown. Jesus is lifted up on the cross—the King enthroned.

For further consideration...

> The same mouths that exclaimed "Hosanna!" are capable of crying "Barabbas!"

Lent V
Strip
Scourge
Mock

Monday 5

Lamentations 4:6

For the chastisement of my people has been greater than the punishment of Sodom, which was overthrown in a moment, though no hand was laid on it.

Simon of Cyrene:

…I'm a passerby, an annual visitor along with countrymen from Cyrene for many successive years, an outsider, but of the Jewish faith. But as a passerby and, briefly, as a bystander, I watched the sorry procession, the agitated soldiers anxious to speed along the men with their burdens of death. The weakest stumbled and fell. He had already been badly bruised by other means, and on his head was a halo of thorns—in all his pain he seemed to wear it as a crown, gently mocking the mockers. He was extraordinary. He reached my point in the crowd and tripped again. A soldier made a beeline for me: perhaps I was the tallest, the shortest, or the darkest—it matters not. I was temporarily conscripted to aid this man to Golgotha. My annoyance at this peremptory treatment subsided on even closer inspection of this man. What had he done? I had heard rumors about him, but they were rumors about a ruler, not about a criminal. A few yards ahead a woman rushed out from the crowd to mop the man's brow. She stepped back and looked at her handkerchief. I shifted the weight of the base of the cross from one shoulder to the other as best I could. I was already bruised. To encourage me, the soldier showed me his cat-o'-nine-tails.

I continued to follow the bent and crouching figure until we reached the place of execution. Did I help him? I hardly think so. I was relieved of my temporary duty and told to go. Then, in a moment of exquisite poignancy, the poor, condemned man turned and thanked me.

I feel that I ought to have remained with the man to be of some comfort to him. Instead, I am returning to the city, while behind me I know that duties are being performed that will lead to his death. I resolve to seek out the man's followers. What sort of teacher was he? What was his message?

Psalm 22

Save me from the mouth of the lion! From the horns of the wild oxen you have rescued me.

Reflection

Pilate abdicates responsibility. Jesus is sentenced as a criminal, taking the place of the criminal, Barabbas. Jesus remains steadfast, in perfect obedience living out his mission in the world. By his steadfastness Jesus is victorious over all the double-dealing, falsity, and hypocrisy. This is the light shining in the darkness—a darkness that cannot overcome—of which St. John wrote at the beginning of his Gospel.

For further consideration...

Can we absolve ourselves from responsibility for our actions merely by saying so?

Tuesday 5

Lamentations 5:1, 2

*Remember, O L*ORD*, what has befallen us; look, and see our disgrace! Our inheritance has been turned over to strangers, our homes to aliens.*

The Beloved Disciple:

The soldiers who are keeping us at a distance have moved a step forward to receive instructions. One is being asked to assist with the second cross. He is slightly reluctant because his duties have not been at all strenuous so far. Instinctively, Mary and I move nearer the Master's body. Now I see the emphatic words of the indictment, which is no indictment at all: "Jesus of Nazareth, King of the Jews." It is as though Pontius Pilate were saying to Caiaphas, "You demanded his blood; remember his blood is that of a king." The paradox weighs heavily, and with more Roman grunts and prisoner's screams the second cross rises, sways, and is now secured.

The two crosses seem to beckon the horizontal cross of Jesus with the chilling words, "You cannot escape;

your place is here with us." And so it is: the gap between the crosses will soon be filled.

The craftsman returns to his duty.

Psalm 22

> *I will tell of your name to my brothers and sisters; in the midst of the congregation I will praise you.*

Reflection

Jesus is a king, though not a king in the sense that Pilate understands. The religious leaders respond to Pilate by urging that the only king they have is Caesar. And yet, St. John wants us to see that, yes, indeed, here is a king. But earlier, when Pilate says, "Behold the man," St. John wishes us to hear, "Behold *the* man"—the proper, true man, the very pattern of what man, made in the image of God, was meant to be.

For further consideration...

> By his kiss, Judas is, in effect, saying to the mob: "Behold the man." Pilate presents Jesus with those very words.

Wednesday 5

Lamentations 5:3–5

We have become orphans, fatherless; our mothers are like widows. We must pay for the water we drink; the wood we get must be bought. With a yoke on our necks we are hard driven; we are weary, we are given no rest.

The Beloved Disciple:

Another flat-headed nail has been selected and is being spun in the air and caught by the craftsman as if to lighten the occasion. But he is indifferent to and remote from the scene. He is kneeling to secure the Master's right arm. Now the world's embrace is there again, about to be fixed for all time. Can this really be the terrible defeat it seems if he really did say—I am sure he did—"Those who have seen me have seen the Father" and, "I am in the Father and Father is in me"?

Three more hammer blows: "Strip! Scourge! Mock!" they now say, and the recent horrors come again to mind. "The King of the Jews," they tell us after they have stripped him, whipped him, and mocked him. Mary stares.

Psalm 22

> *You who fear the Lord, praise him! All you offspring of Jacob, glorify him; stand in awe of him, all you offspring of Israel!*

Reflection

Jesus is dressed in a robe—a cloak of one of the soldiers—and a painful, ludicrous crown, in mock kingship. The soldiers' games simply underline the truth of his kingship.

For further consideration...

In the enjoyment of another's helplessness, we reveal ours.

Thursday 5

Lamentations 5:6–7

*We have made a pact with Egypt and Assyria,
to get enough bread. Our ancestors sinned;
they are no more, and we bear their iniquities.*

The Beloved Disciple:

His palms are filling with blood and he has called upon the Father to forgive his executioners. "They don't know what they do," he has just added. Will the Father now come, or is he here already? With one or two more nails the craftsman's job will be done. He will go away satisfied with his day's work. He will be paid well. Will he be touched by the generosity of his victim in word and in deed? I too ask God to forgive. Do *I* forgive, though?

The soldiers, encouraged by the spectators, had enjoyed their mockery of the Master. They loved their thorny crown and that they could strike and whip a king. The Temple servants enjoyed it too. "Who hit you?" "If you are a half-decent prophet, you could tell me my name." Someone found a piece of scarlet cloth to make the scene even more grotesque. The prophets of old were violently rejected when they pronounced upon matters close to the heart.

The Master sighs.

Psalm 22

> *For he did not despise or abhor the affliction of the afflicted; he did not hide his face from me, but heard, when I cried to him.*

Reflection

We are bidden to take up our cross and follow him. "Christ leads me through no darker room than he went through before," wrote Richard Baxter.

To share in the Easter victory is to share in a love that turns all situations of despair into hope, all places of darkness into light, the destruction of death into endless life. But the way to that victory is the way of the cross, and we cannot know the life that God offers us without entering into the meaning of the cross; without learning something of the way that suffering can be redemptive and transforming. We are baptized into the dying of Jesus. In the broken bread and outpoured wine of the Eucharist we are sustained by the life and love that is at the very heart of Jesus' dying. We cannot escape from the cross as the measure of our Christian faith and our Christian life.

FOR FURTHER CONSIDERATION…

    Simon takes up the Master's cross in an effort to show us our vocation.

Friday 5

Lamentations 5:8–9

Slaves rule over us; there is no one to deliver us from their hand. We get our bread at the peril of our lives, because of the sword in the wilderness.

The Beloved Disciple:

In asking the Father to forgive, has Jesus also forgiven? He forgives and the Father forgives. "The Father is in me and I in him," he said.

Even so, these things make little sense to us—two forlorn spectators, soon to be mourners, on a hill outside Jerusalem—one a friend and disciple, the other a mother who brought him up and nurtured him and stayed faithful to his mission to this very point. Even now, does she still have faith in that mission? If so, what does she expect will happen? What do I expect?

The space between the thieves demands to be occupied. It urges the craftsman to continue his infuriatingly methodical work, finish the task, and go home.

One of the thieves is shouting at Jesus: "Aren't you the Christ? Get us down from here and save yourself!"

There are more people from the Temple now—chief priests and their cohorts, here to gloat at their success.

Psalm 22

> *From you comes my praise in the great*
> *congregation; my vows I will pay*
> *before those who fear him.*

Reflection

Luke brings into the Calvary scene not only the mockers, the voyeurs, the soldiers, and the weeping women of Jerusalem, but also the friends of Jesus and the women who had come with him from Galilee. They were to take their places at a distance from the cross. If we are honest, that is where each one of us is likely to be found. Were the weeping women "official" bewailers of the condemned man? Were they loyal followers distraught at the fate of their Master? Were they guilty of collaborating with the baying and fickle crowds?

For further consideration...

"Weep for yourselves. Weep as the foolish virgins might weep when they are told: 'You may not come in, I do not know you.' Weep for yourselves; prepare for the things to come."

Saturday 5

Lamentations 5:10–11

Our skin is black as an oven from the scorching heat of famine. Women are raped in Zion, virgins in the towns of Judah.

The Beloved Disciple:

Looking at Jesus—the mocking, the stripping, and the scourging done—I can see that he has collected and accepted and been crucified with all the venom and vehemence that can be mustered. The chief priests and elders are heaping this upon him on behalf of everyone else. A thief is swearing again, and someone is silencing him. Soon he will be silent to this world.

The craftsman, apparently savoring his final act before the now larger crowd—for effect, I believe—is trying to decide between a long-shafted nail and two shorter ones. Which should he choose? he wonders. I wonder. He is now studying the feet of the Master and kneels beside them, positioning the right upon the left, causing the right leg to be fixed at an awkward and painful angle. He is placing the long nail on the right foot and raising his hammer.

Psalm 22

> *The poor shall eat and be satisfied;*
> *those who seek him shall praise the Lord.*
> *May your hearts live for ever!*

Reflection

God gives himself completely and goes to the uttermost limit, emptying himself in love and humility. The weakness and nakedness of the child of Bethlehem shows us the same love as the scourged and naked man to be nailed to the rough wood of the cross.

For further consideration...

It is appropriate now to consider the Incarnation paralleled by our Lord's real presence in the Blessed Sacrament.

Holy Week
Flesh
Bone
Wood

Monday of Holy Week

Lamentations 3:13–15

He shot into my vitals the arrows of his quiver; I have become the laughing-stock of all my people, an object of their taunt-songs all day long. He has filled me with bitterness, he has glutted me with wormwood.

The Centurion:

I have seen many an execution. This man in the middle is different from the rest. He is not your run-of-the-mill criminal. Even the authorities have stirred up a fuss because the governor insisted on wording the indictment personally. They wanted this death. Why? It strikes me as odd. He seems to be a decent kind of person. A colleague of mine actually had some dealings with him: It seems this man cured my colleague's servant of some ailment or other. This man seems to have preached that the Jewish God is a paternal God who cares for all creation. (Dare I question whether the Roman gods are make-believe, the art of an ingenious sculptor?) Why should the Temple staff be so determined to rid themselves of him? They could have used him to their advantage, I should have thought. Perhaps they recognized the truth of what he preached and what he was, and were frightened. I know what fear can do—fear of all types.

I see his mother there; she is comforting him by her presence. I will have to stay to the end; there is something remarkable about it all, and I've seen many a crucifixion.

Psalm 22

> *All the ends of the earth shall remember and turn to the* Lord*; and all the families of the nations shall worship before him.*

Reflection

Jesus' kingship and authority is the kingship and authority of love. He redeems through suffering. He makes himself vulnerable sharing our weakness that he might raise us up to share in his life and to live by his same love. The king enthroned on the cross comes into his kingdom of love; we are those who are called to live by the laws of love in that kingdom.

For further consideration...

For the moment, the centurion stands aloof. Something will soon nudge him out of his detachment.

Tuesday of Holy Week

Lamentations 3:16–18

He has made my teeth grind on gravel, and made me cower in ashes; my soul is bereft of peace; I have forgotten what happiness is; so I say, "Gone is my glory, and all that I had hoped for from the LORD."

The Beloved Disciple:

And so, three last hammer blows: "Flesh! Bone! Wood!" No longer does my memory need to be prompted by the past. The hammer now tells us of the reality of the passage of the nail as it penetrates the flesh and pushes the bones aside, securing itself in the wood. The Master is there, pinned to a tree. Soon the craftsman will gather his tools into his bag and leave the scene, a job well done.

The centurion, almost in sorrow—but I probably only imagine it—is now directing his soldiers to rope the cross, guide the foot, and haul. The cross is rising slowly—it carries a greater burden than the weight of the Master—and now drops into its shaft with a jolt.

Jesus stretches his neck and closes his eyes for a moment. The three crosses are together.

I am moving forward with Mary to the foot of the cross; the other Marys and Salome are moving also.

Psalm 22

> *For dominion belongs to the Lord,*
> *and he rules over the nations.*

Reflection

The label informs everyone: it is written in the language of the learned man of the Temple, of the Roman, of the common man. Pilate, who has washed his hands of Jesus and of the truth, decrees that the label should be left as he has drafted it.

The cross of a criminal is the throne of Jesus' tortured body.

For further consideration...

> Language is no barrier to the declaration of kingship; there is no barrier between the cross and humankind.

Wednesday of Holy Week

Lamentations 1:16

For these things I weep; my eyes flow with tears; for a comforter is far from me, one to revive my courage; my children are desolate, for the enemy has prevailed.

The Beloved Disciple

Does despair create fantasy? Is the Master not the epitome of a king, reigning over us from on high? Few would see it; his followers' tears do not support it. Having been lifted high on the cross on earth, shall he be lifted high in heaven? That is where he is going—to the Father, where we cannot yet follow.

The less aggressive thief has just admonished the other and has said to Jesus: "Remember me when you come into your kingdom." He is replying: "Today you shall be with me in Paradise." Does that mean more than a relief from pain? Can a thief travel with him where a disciple cannot? Will there be work for us to do here without the Master?

Mary is looking up at her Son and he returns the gaze, addressing her with difficulty. "Mother, look, your son," he is saying; as he turns his head toward me: "Look, your mother."

Psalm 22

> *To him, indeed, shall all who sleep in the*
> *earth bow down; before him shall bow all who*
> *go down to the dust, and I shall live for him.*

Reflection

We are wounded disciples following a wounded Savior, but we follow in the power of his Spirit who is the transfigurer of our wounds. "There is no such thing as an unscarred saint," wrote Father Andrew of the Society of the Divine Compassion. And there are only two things we can do with these wounds, which we all bear: we can allow them to fester, or we can offer them to be cauterized and transfigured in the healing love of Christ.

For further consideration…

Hanging next to God the Son, the thief asks to be remembered. He asks only that. He does not aspire any higher. He is rewarded with more. How full of meaning is that "remember me"?

Holy Thursday

Lamentations 2:19

Arise, cry out in the night, at the beginning of the watches! Pour out your heart like water before the presence of the Lord! Lift your hands to him for the lives of your children, who faint with hunger at the head of every street.

The Beloved Disciple:

I am to care for her as my own mother. How could I not do so? I place my arm around his mother to show him my response. He bleeds over the remnant of his followers and over his mother, now my mother.

Even at this late stage there are cries, cruel and mocking cries, from officials and the others who wish to enjoy the end. The Master is in prayer to the Father, and I hear him recite a psalm that begins by recalling despair and ends in gladness. Each of his final moments seems to have a purpose in providing the finishing touches to his ministry. He now thirsts and is saying as much, and someone is offering him the traditional sponge of sour wine held to his lips on a stake. It is said to dull the pain. His devoted follower, Mary of Magdala, is crying copiously as she senses that the Master is making his final preparations.

Psalm 22

> *Posterity will serve him; future generations will be told about the Lord....*

Reflection

Christian devotion through the ages has placed the cross, in many different forms, on altars and on steeples. The cross is planted at the very heart of our faith. It is *the* Christian sign; a Christianity without the cross is no Christianity at all. The early Christians looked around the world and, with the eye of faith, saw the cross imprinted on the very fabric of human lives and on the world as God's creation. They looked at ships crossing the sea and saw the mast and yardarm from which the sail hung as the figure of the cross; they looked at their primitive plows and saw again the figure of the cross; they looked into the heavens and saw the planets and stars revolving around each other, forming the figure of a cross. They meditated on barriers between heaven and earth and Jew and Gentile as forming a cross, which Christ had transformed from a cross of separation into one of unity.

FOR FURTHER CONSIDERATION...
>
> The complete and all-embracing love for humankind is summed up in "Behold, your Mother."

Good Friday

Lamentations 3:19; 2:18

The thought of my affliction and my homelessness is wormwood and gall! Cry aloud to the Lord! O wall of daughter Zion! Let tears stream down like a torrent day and night! Give yourself no rest, your eyes no respite!

Mary:

My Son, my Son, I am here. I am with you. But why this suffering; why such a death? I cannot bear it. Is this your Father's business, which Joseph and I failed to understand when we lost you all those years ago in the Temple?

I have prayed to the Father, but how can he be named as a loving Father and called "Abba" when this is what happens: this torture, this bleeding, this wracking pain? And yet…and yet, I still hold on to that promise at your coming, and still I whisper the response of faith: Be it done to me according to your word. And still I plead: Lord, I believe, help my unbelief.

First Thief:

Oh, the pain, the agony! Let's get it over with quickly. Hardly worth it, that stuff we stole. It wasn't much, and they get rid of us like this, lumped together with this crazy man who thinks he's some kind of a prophet. How's it feel now? Stupid fool!

Second Thief:

For heaven's sake, don't make it worse. You never know.... This man might really be who he says he is.... Lord, remember me when you come into your kingdom.

Our Lord:

Father, forgive them, they do not know what they are doing. Father, if it be your will, let this cup pass from me; nevertheless, not my will but yours be done. Father, the darkness presses upon me: the darkness of the sky; the darkness of this pain; the darkness of betrayal, loneliness, abandonment. Father, how dark, how heavy is this weight of evil. Father, your love is the light of life, but where are you? Where is that love, that knowledge of your presence, that delight in your care? My God, my God, I cry to you in agony and pain, out of the depths of hell, from the darkness of death. My God, my God, why have you forsaken me? With pierced hands and feet, with wounded heart, out of the deep I call to you, O Lord; Lord, hear my voice. Lord, I thirst, thirst for your presence; my Father, for all you have given me, for the life of the world. Into your hands I commend my spirit, for it is finished, perfected, completed.

The Beloved Disciple:

Mary is resolute. She will remain until he breathes his last and is taken down for burial. I will remain with her. A few moments ago he cried out and said that his mission was complete. It becomes clearer to me as time passes that this really must be part of it, though there is no feeling of triumph and success in my soul. We had no wish to contemplate the uncomfortable and the unpleasant when he gave those warnings and accurate predictions.

The craftsman is on his way home. The thieves are quiet, but still a long way from death; the Master is close to it. He is opening his mouth to speak and is summoning up strength. He is commending himself to God. His head now droops, and I think he is dead. Mary's head droops also. There is a numbness, a blankness, though everything around me is the same. The bodies will be removed quickly after the soldiers have made sure that all are dead.

The centurion has made an unexpected remark, which reminds me that at the Master's baptism in the Jordan a voice from heaven said roughly the same thing.

Psalm 22

> *Future generations will be told about the*
> *Lord, and proclaim his deliverance to a people*
> *yet unborn, saying that he has done it.*

Reflection

As we stand on the hill of Calvary and edge toward the foot of the cross, we look at our Lord hanging there in agony and pain. This is the mirror for us of the love of God. God loves and cares for us, so individually—in all our needs, in our weakness, and in our strength—that he enters into our condition and knows it from the inside. He redeems through suffering; he makes himself vulnerable and shares our weakness that he might raise us up to share in his life and live by his same love. The Christ who died is the Christ who was raised to life for us, and is raised to life in us: Good Friday and Easter belong together.

For further consideration…

We can consider matters only in the knowledge of the Resurrection and our redemption, because we are Easter people.

Prayer

Lord, you were nailed to the cross for love of me. You knew from the inside our human pain, our burden of sin, the world's evil. You knew injustice, betrayal, and abandonment. You knew, like us, the absence of your Father in the darkness; and yet in that darkness he was with you, so that out of every hell you have redeemed humankind. We adore you, O Christ, and we bless you, because by your holy cross you have redeemed the world. You, Christ, are the King of Glory; crowned with thorns you reign in triumph, lifted high on the cross. We worship your great love and praise you for your glory. Amen.

Holy Saturday

Lamentations 5:21, 22

Restore us to yourself, O L<small>ORD</small>, that we may be restored; renew our days as of old—unless you have utterly rejected us, and are angry with us beyond measure.

The Beloved Disciple:

Jesus is dead. A soldier has just made sure of it with the thrust of his spear, the spear whose shaft restrained Mary and restrained me earlier in the day. With sickening barbarity, the others are being finished off.

The miracle at Cana again comes to mind. That was his beginning and this is his end. The outpouring of water changed into wine warned of the outpouring of the cup of wine not so many hours ago, and of his blood today. Is there comfort in that? Not yet. We are bereft, and there is now a hollowness and emptiness.

We shall bury the Master and lay the temple that is his body in a tomb, there to remain….

Psalm 93

> *The floods have lifted up, O Lord, the floods*
> *have lifted up their voice; the floods lift up*
> *their roaring. More majestic than the thunders*
> *of mighty waters, more majestic than the*
> *waves of the sea, majestic on high is the Lord!*

Reflection

Today, Holy Saturday, or the Easter vigil, is surely the most mysterious day of the Christian calendar, and yet all too rarely do Christians pause to consider its significance. Time, thought, and energy are taken up with the decoration of churches for Easter. Poised between the darkness of Good Friday and the light of Easter, it is a day of profound silence. "Christ suffered, died, and was buried." Today the Christ of God is with the dead, eliminated from the world, knowing death as completely and absolutely as each one of us will eventually know death.

The Gospel records of the Passion tell of the agony of Gethsemane—a shrinking from the costly demand of redemptive love. They speak of a darkness over the land on Good Friday that is more than physical, a dark inner engulfing of meaning and purpose. They place on the lips of Jesus the powerful opening words of Psalm 22 that speaks of the desiccating torture as life ebbs away.

He not only died, the Creed affirms that "he descended into hell." Strictly speaking, this is Hades (or the Hebrew *She'ol*), the place of wraith-like existence of the departed. Part of the stumbling-block of Christianity is that the God who was revealed in Jesus is a God who goes to the uttermost limits, into the very nothingness of death. And God goes into that nothingness through a descent into the hell of unmeaning. The cry of dereliction on the lips of the crucified is terrifying. If incarnation is real, if God engages so radically with the world as to know the world's evil and our human mortality from the inside, God chooses to experience and encompass a world without God and so without ultimate meaning. He descended into the hell that is apartness from God, into the hell of the absence of God, into the hell of impotent rage against God, into the silence of the grave. The twisted, tortured figure clamped by crude nails to the wood of the cross is where the God who is love goes to the uttermost. There the evil and suffering of the world, which was created with the terrible freedom to love and to deny love, is known from the inside. Here, says Lancelot Andrewes, "the very book of charity is laid open before us."

In the nineteenth century, Hegel wrote that "the human, the finite, the fragile, the weak, the negative are themselves a moment of the divine; they are within God himself." The psalmist, centuries earlier, had reached out in faith to affirm, "If I go down to hell, you are there also." In the early centuries of the Church, the Christian imagination sought to express in vivid pictures this free choosing of God to know and be found in the darkness. The apocryphal gospel of Nicodemus dramatically describes the encounter in the realm of the dead between Christ and the powers of darkness who held the departed captive. The walls of hell fall like the walls of Jericho, and the prisoners are set free. Here is the basis for the harrowing-of-hell scenes in countless medieval passion plays, in which the archetypal conflict of good and evil, of life and death, is as popular as it is in the cinema of the twentieth century.

"He descended into hell"—the silence of Holy Saturday takes Good Friday to the uttermost limit, and it is from that silence of the grave, and the darkness of evil triumphant, that Christ is raised to the life of God's new creation. History is broken open to the life of the world to come, and the reign of the love that death could not hold is the kingdom of God that the Easter Gospel proclaims. The icons of Eastern Christendom portray the Resurrection not, as in medieval Western painting, showing Christ stepping out of a tomb, but as Christ's triumph over the imprisoning powers of darkness. One of the most powerful of these images, in the Church of St. Savior in Chora, Istanbul, shows Christ in a shimmering circle of glory. His hands are outstretched, drawing Adam and Eve—representing all humanity—from death to life, from the old order to the new. Beneath his feet the bolts and bars of hell lie shattered. The prisoners are set free, the demons are fallen, and life reigns. It is no wonder that in St. Mark's Gospel the women run from the empty tomb in terror.

FOR FURTHER CONSIDERATION…

Do we always think carefully before we speak or act, so that our words and deeds never have the effect of the soldier's spear?

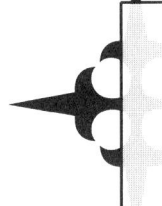

The Day of Resurrection
Christ Is Risen

Easter Morning

Lamentations 5:19

*But you, O Lord, reign for ever;
your throne endures to all generations.*

Reflection

Easter is an explosion—a stunning, overwhelming, surprising event that blows our human history wide open and transforms our expectations. Dead men are dead. Bodies rot in the ground. When a life is over, the person may live in our memory, but that is all. But Easter is not like that; it turns the world upside down, for God has done a new thing, a surpassing, wonderful, new thing. It is not surprising that Gospel accounts of the Resurrection of Jesus are all clear that something new and surprising has happened, but the accounts stumble and vary over the details. Who goes to the tomb first? Who first encounters the Risen Jesus? There are appearances in Jerusalem and appearances in Galilee. And yet, all the Easter stories in the Gospels (and St. Paul's witness in his letters) home in on one single, rich, and amazing truth: Christ is risen and Jesus is alive. The cross is not, therefore, the end, because death is conquered. This Resurrection, this new life, this new creation, is a life to be shared.

The poet Gerard Manley Hopkins talks about Christ "Eastering" in us. That reminds us powerfully that Easter—the Resurrection—is for Christians something active, alive, and transforming, and not something unusual that happened in the past. Easter life is something we share here and now, but something we share in its completeness only at the final fulfillment of God's purposes. St. Paul puts it like this: "As in Adam all die, so in Christ shall all be made alive." Easter, for all the Gospels, is not just about Jesus, but about the disciples; not just about all the disciples, but about all Christians; not just about all Christians, but about us. From now on we are Easter people, and alleluia (Praise be to God) is our song.

Alleluia, Christ is Risen!

He is risen indeed, Alleluia!

Prayer

> Christ, who is sinless, reconciles sinners to the Father.
> Death and life have contended in that combat
>   stupendous:
> the Prince of Life, who died, reigns immortal.

Christ indeed from death is risen, our new life
   securing:
have mercy, victor King, ever reigning.
   Amen. Alleluia.

—Based on the Easter Sequence

O Risen Lord, secure in me the knowledge of your forgiving mercy, the comfort of your redeeming love, and the joy of your all-powerful Resurrection from the dead. Give me the strength to take up my cross and follow you to the heavenly realms where you reign in glory with the Father and the Holy Spirit throughout all ages. Amen.

Psalm 93

*The Lord is king, he is robed in majesty;
the Lord is robed, he is girded with strength.
He has established the world; it shall never be
moved; your throne is established from of old;
you are from everlasting. Your decrees are
very sure; holiness befits your house, O Lord,
for evermore.*

About the Authors

Geoffrey Rowell, the Bishop of Gibraltar in Europe, is the author of numerous academic and devotional works.

Julien Chilcott-Monk, a writer and musician, is the author of a number of devotional works.

Pauline BOOKS & MEDIA

The Daughters of St. Paul operate book and media centers at the following addresses. Visit, call or write the one nearest you today, or find us on the World Wide Web, www.pauline.org

CALIFORNIA

3908 Sepulveda Blvd, Culver City, CA 90230   310-397-8676

5945 Balboa Avenue, San Diego, CA 92111   858-565-9181

46 Geary Street, San Francisco, CA 94108   415-781-5180

FLORIDA

145 SW 107th Avenue, Miami, FL 33174   305-559-6715

HAWAII

1143 Bishop Street, Honolulu, HI 96813   808-521-2731

Neighbor Islands call: 800-259-8463

ILLINOIS

172 North Michigan Avenue, Chicago, IL 60601
312-346-4228

LOUISIANA

4403 Veterans Memorial Blvd, Metairie, LA 70006   504-887-7631

MASSACHUSETTS

885 Providence Hwy, Dedham, MA 02026   781-326-5385

MISSOURI

9804 Watson Road, St. Louis, MO 63126   314-965-3512

NEW JERSEY

561 U.S. Route 1, Wick Plaza, Edison, NJ 08817   732-572-1200

NEW YORK

150 East 52nd Street, New York, NY 10022   212-754-1110

78 Fort Place, Staten Island, NY 10301   718-447-5071

PENNSYLVANIA

9171-A Roosevelt Blvd, Philadelphia, PA 19114   215-676-9494

SOUTH CAROLINA

243 King Street, Charleston, SC 29401   843-577-0175

TENNESSEE

4811 Poplar Avenue, Memphis, TN 38117   901-761-2987

TEXAS

114 Main Plaza, San Antonio, TX 78205   210-224-8101

VIRGINIA

1025 King Street, Alexandria, VA 22314   703-549-3806

CANADA

3022 Dufferin Street, Toronto, Ontario, Canada M6B 3T5   416-781-9131

1155 Yonge Street, Toronto, Ontario, Canada M4T 1W2   416-934-3440

¡También somos su fuente para libros, videos y música en español!